Piranhas

Piranhas

Melissa Gish

Living Wild

CREATIVE EDUCATION
CREATIVE PAPERBACKS

Published by Creative Education and Creative Paperbacks
P.O. Box 227, Mankato, Minnesota 56002
Creative Education and Creative Paperbacks are imprints of
The Creative Company
www.thecreativecompany.us

Book design and production by Graham Morgan (www.bluedes.com)
Art direction by Rita Marshall
Edited by Joe Tischler

Photographs by 2009 MCT (Mark Randall), Alamy (blickwinkel, Larry Larsen),
Dreamstime (Bonita Chestier, Chrishowey, Lightpoet, Liubomirt, Alexander
Mironov, Jiri Vaclavek, King Ho Yim), Getty (Tony Allen, Chris Catton, Mark
Smith), iStock (itsme23), National Geographic Creative (Imacon X5, Joel
Sartore), Pexels (Guryan), Public Domain (Marcus Elieser Bloch, Robert H.
Schomburgk), Shutterstock (guentermanaus, Janne Hamalainen, lightpoet),
Unsplash (Anton Darius, Lorisha Buhler Ferrara, Adam Smigielski), Wikimedia
Commons (Ltshears, Public Domain)

Library of Congress Cataloging-in-Publication Data
Names: Gish, Melissa, author.
Title: Piranhas / by Melissa Gish.
Description: Mankato, Minnesota : Creative Education and Creative
    Paperbacks, [2024] | Series: Living wild | Includes bibliographical references
    and index. | Audience: Ages 10–14 | Audience: Grades 7–9 | Summary:
    "Brimming with photos and scientific facts, Piranhas treats middle-grade
    researchers and wild animal lovers to a comprehensive zoological profile
    of this fearsome freshwater fish. Includes sidebars, a range map, a glossary,
    and a Brazilian piranha tale"—Provided by publisher.
Identifiers: LCCN 2022043746 (print) | LCCN 2022043747 (ebook) | ISBN
    9781640266070 (library binding) | ISBN 9781682771624 (paperback) | ISBN
    9781640007260 (ebook)
Subjects: LCSH: Piranhas—Juvenile literature.
Classification: LCC QL638.C5 G57 2024 (print) | LCC QL638.C5 (ebook) | DDC
    597/.48—dc23/eng/20220913
LC record available at https://lccn.loc.gov/2022043746
LC ebook record available at https://lccn.loc.gov/2022043747

Printed in China

CONTENTS

It is early April in Venezuela's Orinoco Delta, and only scattered pools of water remain in the once-flooded forest. The five-month drought has trapped four red-bellied piranhas in a shrinking pool. The fish have consumed all the smaller fish, crustaceans, and insects in their small habitat. With starvation looming, they are desperate for a meal. They swim nervously in circles, darting here and there. In the distance, thunder rumbles, signaling the coming rain. If the piranhas do not eat soon, they will not survive long enough to enjoy the rainy season's flooding of the forest once again. Suddenly, a frog leaps into the pool. In an instant, a hundred tiny teeth skewer the frog's body. The water churns as the piranhas feast. They devour everything—even bone. Within minutes the pool is still again, its smooth surface disturbed only by the first raindrops of the season.

One way to check a piranha's teeth without damaging the fish is by pulling back the lips.

Take a Bite

Piranhas have a reputation for ferocity that makes them known and feared worldwide, yet they are confined to the continent of South America.

Piranhas belong to the Characidae family of fish, which contains more than 1,200 species, including the common tetras, which are popular aquarium fish.

As members of the subfamily Serrasalmidae, piranhas are most closely related to pacus (*pa-KOOS*) and silver dollars. Like piranhas, these fish are **endemic** to South America and can live both in the wild and in aquariums. Pacus and silver dollars resemble piranhas in general appearance; however, pacus grow three times larger than piranhas, and silver dollars reach less than 6 inches (15 centimeters) in length—smaller than even the smallest piranha. Both pacus and silver dollars have flat teeth designed for eating vegetation, unlike piranhas, whose teeth are incredibly sharp.

The name "piranha" is derived from two words in the language of the Guaraní Indians: *pirá*, meaning "fish," and *ranha*, meaning "tooth." While the exact number of piranha species is unconfirmed, scientists estimate that up to 60 different species may exist. Many of these fish are named for their colors, including the red-bellied, gold, black, and blue-tiger piranhas. The rhombeus piranha is named for the shape of its scales, which are rhombuses, or diamonds.

About 15 million years ago, the first piranha ancestors **evolved** to develop the jutting lower jaws and razor-sharp teeth that are the defining characteristics of modern piranhas. Piranhas are oval shaped and dorsolaterally compressed, which means that, when viewed head-on, they appear to have a flattened body. Piranhas vary in size and color, but most have olive to grayish-green or grayish-blue bodies. They have different colored bellies, gills, and tails that vary by species. One of the smallest piranha species is the iridescent piranha. This silvery green fish with tiny black spots grows to about 7 inches (18 cm) in length. One of the largest piranhas, the São Francisco piranha, which has shimmering orange and yellow scales on its belly, can reach 24 inches (61 cm) and weigh up to 13 pounds (6 kilograms). Most piranha species are the size of the red-bellied piranha. This fish grows to about 13 inches (33 cm) and 3 pounds (1.4 kg).

In the wild, piranhas live in tropical fresh water that is 75 to 80 degrees Fahrenheit (24 to 27 degrees Celsius). They cannot survive in water that is too cold, so they are not found in mountainous environments or areas where cold mountain streams could flood their habitat. While they can be found in most lakes, lagoons, and waterways throughout South America, from Colombia

Red-bellied piranhas live in the Amazon River.

Where in the World They Live

The nearly 60 species of piranha inhabit only tropical fresh waters throughout the northern half of South America, and many species are found in such major rivers as the Amazon, Orinoco, and São Francisco. The six species shown represent some of the more prevalent piranha species.

2. Blue-Tiger Piranha: Amazon and Orinoco river basins

1. Gold Piranha: South American rivers

6. Black Shoulder Piranha: Orinoco River basin

5. Black Piranha: South American rivers (especially in Guyana)

4. Red-Bellied Piranha: South American rivers (Including Amazon)

3. Violet Line Piranha:
Brazilian rivers

Estimated to be between 1,500 and 1,700 miles (2,414–2,736 kilometers) long, the Orinoco is South America's second-longest river.

to northern Argentina, their largest habitats are the Orinoco River in Venezuela and the Amazon and São Francisco Rivers in Brazil. Smaller piranhas typically remain in areas where food is abundant, such as weedy ponds, but larger piranha species will roam rivers and streams to hunt.

Like all fish, piranhas breathe through slits in their bodies called gills. As a piranha swims, water is forced through the gills, where thin membranes collect oxygen and transfer it to the piranha's bloodstream. While some piranhas are constantly on the move, others wait to ambush prey. Like most bony fish, piranhas have a swim bladder, which is a gas-filled sac, or pouch, that regulates the fish's buoyancy, keeping it afloat when it isn't moving. In this way, piranhas can hide among water plants and wait for prey to approach them. They are speedy and can attack unsuspecting prey with virtually no warning, biting so quickly and so deeply that the victim often bleeds to death before being fully devoured by its attacker.

The piranha's body is covered with slime that protects it from disease. This slime, produced by glands beneath the piranha's scales, also cuts the resistance to the water flowing over the fish as it swims. This feature helps piranhas swim more quickly and with more agility than other fish. In addition, piranhas have five different kinds of fins that help them move swiftly. Paired pectoral fins behind the gills are used for vertical movement and steering. The dorsal fin on the back stabilizes the piranha. The ventral and anal fins on the lower body also keep piranhas from rolling over. The caudal, or tail, fin helps propel a piranha forward. As members of the Characidae family, piranhas also have a small, thick fin near the tail. This fin, called the adipose fin, stores fat that a piranha can rely on when food is scarce.

A piranha's most characteristic feature is its set of wide, triangular-shaped teeth that are designed to shear chunks of meat from prey. Like a human interlocking their fingers, the piranha's top teeth fit into the spaces between the bottom teeth. The piranha also has an underbite, which means its lower jaw extends past its upper jaw. This feature allows the piranha to take bigger bites than other types of fish its size. Piranha teeth are arranged in a single row. As teeth are broken or worn down, replacement teeth grow upward from the gum. Piranhas may go through hundreds of teeth in a lifetime.

Piranhas have keen eyesight. Their large eyes allow them to see prey from the front and the sides. They also have a powerful sense of smell. The blood of a wounded animal will draw piranhas from up to 2 miles (3.2 km) away.

A piranha's nostrils, covered by nasal flaps called nares, lead to highly sensitive organs related to its sense of smell.

Piranhas also rely on their unique form of hearing to locate prey that is splashing in the water. The first four pairs of bones in the piranha's back just below its skull make up its **auditory** system. Called the Weberian apparatus, this system connects the bones to the swim bladder and inner ear, which helps the piranha hear splashes in the form of vibrations or sound waves detected by changes in pressure. The skin of a piranha also has many tiny pores that lead to small sense organs inside its body called the lateral line system. These organs detect movement and pressure changes, alerting the piranha to splashing as well as helping it know when to speed up, slow down, change direction, or right itself in the water.

From Fry to Ferocious

Some piranha species, such as the black piranha, are solitary creatures, but most other species (including the violet line, black shoulder, and green piranhas) swim in large groups called shoals.

Scientists once believed that piranhas gathered in shoals to hunt, but recent research has proven otherwise. Particularly during seasonal changes, when piranha predators such as **caimans** and river dolphins are most active, many species of piranhas gather in shoals of as many as 1,000 individuals for the sole purpose of staying alive in their murky, muddy habitats.

Piranhas have a greater chance of being eaten by a larger animal than of successfully attacking one. When shoals move through the water as one large unit, juvenile piranhas swim near the center, where they are further protected. In areas of shallow water, piranhas are vulnerable to birds such as herons. Caimans, gliding silently through the water, can easily snatch piranhas from the outer edge of a shoal. In the deep, larger fish such as pirarucu (*pih-RAH-rih-koo*) regularly feed on piranhas.

Some piranhas are carnivores and feed mainly on meat; however, most piranhas are **omnivorous**. Adults must eat at least every other day, and juveniles must eat several times each day. The search for food is a piranha's strongest instinct, and piranhas do little else throughout their lives. Piranhas hunt live prey, but they are also scavengers. They feed on dead fish and other animals, thus performing the important **ecological** service of helping to maintain the cleanliness and health of their habitat. Many piranha species, despite having a mouthful of teeth capable of shredding flesh, subsist on a diet made up mostly of seeds and fruit that fall into the water. The wimple piranha feeds exclusively on the scales of other fish, nibbling at prey without causing lasting injury. This behavior is called lepidophagy (*lep-i-DOF-a-jee*).

Some piranha species actively stalk and kill crustaceans, water insects, and other fish, but most are opportunistic hunters, preying on frogs, snakes, small mammals, or birds that just happen to land in the water. Because piranhas generally do not defend a territory against intruders, piranhas of different species will often feed together. But as they gather to feed, they can rise into a "frenzy," becoming more and more agitated and biting wildly at anything and everything within reach—even each other. For this reason, the **indigenous** people of Venezuela call the piranha *caribe*, a word that means "cannibal," or one who eats the flesh of his own kind.

River otters typically eat about 3 pounds (1.4 kg) of fish—particularly piranhas—each day.

Even the most aggressive piranha species rarely attack large prey if smaller prey is abundant. Starving piranhas can be deadly, however. Three species of piranha are particularly dangerous to humans. These are the black shoulder (or black spot) piranha, the red-bellied piranha, and the São Francisco piranha. While a fatal attack on a human has never been documented, these piranhas have been reported to bite off fingers and toes and take chunks of flesh from victims' legs and hips.

Warmer temperatures trigger the breeding impulse in piranhas. Depending on the species, piranhas spawn, or reproduce, at different times during the rainy season, which usually begins in April. To indicate that they are ready to breed, piranhas' coloration changes. Females change less drastically than males, whose bodies turn dark and whose red, orange, yellow, or purple bellies, gills, and fins grow brighter to attract females. At this time, even solitary species come together to spawn.

Like most fish, piranhas reproduce by laying eggs. In some species, a breeding pair selects an isolated spot, usually in a shallow area near the bank where grasses and weeds are plentiful. The male swishes his body back and forth to clear out a slight impression in the mud or sand. He then coaxes the female to this nest, where she may help him continue to hollow it out. The nest ultimately becomes about 6 inches (15 cm) in diameter and about 2 inches (5 cm) deep.

When they are ready to spawn, the male and female swim in circles around each other for several minutes, and then they swim side by side. With their heads pointed downward, they begin

In the animal kingdom, changing color can signal many things, but for piranhas, it is usually a mating technique.

Although young piranhas'
teeth are only 1/6 inch
(4 millimeters)
long, they are still
potentially deadly.

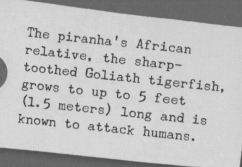

The piranha's African relative, the sharp-toothed Goliath tigerfish, grows to up to 5 feet (1.5 meters) long and is known to attack humans.

releasing eggs and sperm simultaneously—about 30 eggs at a time. They nip each other lightly and slap their tails together. This behavior is repeated numerous times until all 500 to 5,000 eggs are released and fertilized. Spawning takes several hours for species that produce thousands of eggs.

For other piranha species, no nest is created. Rather, the breeding pair simply deposits their eggs in a mass of vegetation to which the sticky eggs adhere. The male aggressively guards the eggs as he fans his tail back and forth to help oxygen flow around the eggs. Because of this attention, more than 90 percent of the young survive to hatch in 2 to 4 days. The tiny fish, called fry, have no eyes or scales. New fry cannot swim. Their slimy little bodies stick to plant roots, where they remain for about a week until the eyes, scales, and fins have developed. Then fry are able to swim around their habitat.

A young piranha's greatest natural threat is a bigger piranha, so juvenile piranhas tend to stay hidden in the roots of floating vegetation until they grow large enough to avoid being considered prey. After several weeks, parents seem to forget their protective breeding instincts and may even try to eat their own young. For the first few months of their lives, piranhas stick together in juvenile

Juvenile piranhas stick close together to increase their chances of surviving an attack by a predator.

shoals, feeding on tiny insects and worms, fruit, and seeds—and sometimes each other—while trying to avoid bigger piranhas.

Juveniles grow quickly, as much as half an inch (1.3 cm) per month. By the time a piranha is about 3 inches (7.6 cm) long, it can defend itself from attacks by other piranhas and will become a member of an adult shoal. The life span of piranhas varies by species, but most can live between 10 and 20 years. Aquarium specimens tend to live much shorter lives than wild piranhas; however, a piranha in Great Britain's Bolton Museum Aquarium was reported to have lived for 23 years when it died in 2000.

Nightmare Fish

Piranhas most likely owe their lasting reputation as bloodthirsty, flesh-shredding monsters to Theodore Roosevelt, the 26th president of the United States.

An adventurer who traveled the world and wrote about his exploits in lively fashion, Roosevelt visited Central and South America in the early 1900s. His Brazilian hosts wanted to make the trip spectacular, so **zoologist** Alipio de Miranda-Ribeiro prepared an event for Roosevelt to witness. He ordered tightly woven nets to be drawn across the Rio Aripuana in two places to isolate a small section of the river, and then he put the local fishermen to work catching piranhas with which to stock the area.

Over the next several days, thousands of piranhas were tossed into the pen. Isolated from their prey, the piranhas grew hungrier every day. When Roosevelt was led to the river where the piranhas were trapped, he was warned to stay out of the water and told that the fish would eat him down to his skeleton. Roosevelt did not believe these words and asked for proof, which Miranda-Ribeiro was well prepared to offer, for he had brought with him to the river a sick, old cow that he planned to sacrifice. He slit the cow's udder with a knife and then drove it into the river. Almost immediately, the fish attacked

São Francisco piranhas, also called piraya piranhas, can be particularly aggressive when seeking prey.

the stumbling, bleeding cow. Leaping from the surging water, they ripped the cow to shreds and devoured it down to the bones. Roosevelt chronicled this and other sights he witnessed in Brazil in his 1914 book *Through the Brazilian Wilderness*, remarking that piranhas were "the most ferocious fish in the world."

The reality, however, is that piranhas are skittish creatures that rarely attack large living prey, preferring instead to scavenge **carcasses** floating in the water. A shoal of piranhas will send a single fish, called a scout, out to a large prey animal to nip at it. If the animal reacts, the shoal usually goes away. If the animal does not react—because it is dead or very near death—the entire shoal will attack. For this reason, shoals of piranhas usually do not attack humans.

People who have coexisted with piranhas for centuries are not afraid of swimming in piranha-infested water.

One scout may bite a person, but the person's reaction to being bitten frightens the shoal away. Native South Americans know this, which is why they are not afraid to swim where well-fed piranhas are present. Piranhas are opportunistic, meaning they will eat when they come upon an easy meal. If food doesn't come easily, smaller piranhas actively search for food in the morning, and bigger piranhas begin searching for food in late afternoon. Native people have learned to work around the piranhas' schedules—and to take advantage of them.

Piranhas often hunt by launching a surprise attack on prey that topples from trees overhanging the water.

Fishermen often use raw meat to bait piranhas, whose powerful scent receptors easily detect the smell of blood.

A popular Brazilian soup made with vegetables, chiles, and ginger root includes piranha heads to increase the eater's physical stamina.

Piranhas are far from the top of the **food chain**. For thousands of years, people have eaten piranhas, as they are among the most abundant and important fish taken from the river systems of South America. Piranha teeth have even been used in making cutting tools and ornaments. **Archaeologists** have found piranha images etched on stones in Brazil and woven into baskets in Paraguay dating back to the 17th century. Carved piranha **totems** and cave drawings more than 600 years old have been found in Venezuela.

In modern North American society, piranhas are typically depicted as having huge, gaping mouths. Playing on this reputation, the family board game *Piranha Panic* requires players to roll dice to move their fish marbles through the Amazon River toward safety as hungry piranhas threaten them along the way. Piranha Plants, cartoonish creations resembling Venus flytraps, are notorious for eating anything that approaches them and are encountered throughout the *Super Mario* series of video games. And *Piranha* is the name of an attack boat that is part of the G.I. Joe action figure line.

In real life, Project 865 Piranha was the name given to the construction of two experimental submarines created by the Russian navy. The subs were designed to be exceptionally small and to maneuver almost silently through the water—just like their namesake. One boat was launched in 1986 and the other in 1990, but neither is in service today. Today, the MOWAG Piranha is a family of armored combat vehicles designed by a Swiss company. The vehicles are used by more than two dozen military forces around the world, including the United States, which added the first Piranha Light Armored Vehicle-25 (LAV-25) to the Marine Corps' fleet of vehicles in 1983, and Brazil and Spain, which use the Piranha III, an **amphibious** vehicle.

In 1960, Dann Deaver, cofounder of Centaur Engineering, designed the Centaur Piranha Cycolac Research Vehicle (CRV), an experimental car whose body was made almost entirely of thermoplastic. This car was featured in the 1960s television series *The Man from U.N.C.L.E.* At the Chicago Auto Show in 2000, General Motors revealed the Pontiac Piranha, an experimental car that its designers called "a small package with a big bite." Although the car was not available for sale to the public, fans of such futuristic vehicles could get a miniature Piranha from the Matchbox toy brand.

Myths about piranhas' ferocity persist, thanks in part to television shows and movies. In 1959, Walt Disney Productions (now known as The Walt Disney Company) sent a group of filmmakers to Brazil to make the film *Jungle Cat*, the story of a jaguar and her cubs. The film featured a glimpse of piranhas in a river. But filmmakers went nowhere near a river. To shoot the scene, fish expert Willi Schwartz first filled a wooden tank with piranhas that had been starved for a week. The camera, from its position in a hole in the tank, recorded the piranhas as they exploded into a feeding frenzy over a small animal dropped into the tank.

Visitors to Venezuela and Colombia have reported that grilled piranha tastes like freshwater trout or perch.

Even more recent films such as 2010's *Mega Piranha* and *Piranha 3D* perpetuate the view of piranhas as ferocious monsters. However, many misconceptions are slowly being dispelled by such TV shows as Animal Planet's *River Monsters*. Host Jeremy Wade caught and released several species of piranha and even joined a shoal of piranhas in a swimming pool—all the while demonstrating that, despite their famous teeth, piranhas are not completely unlike most other fish in the world.

Fishermen often consider piranhas to be a nuisance because their teeth slice through fishing lines as they steal bait meant for other catch.

Animal Tale: The Fish's Teeth

The creatures of the Amazon River have been part of Amazonian cultures' storytelling for thousands of years. This ancient Brazilian tale reveals why certain fish have teeth.

Long ago, fish had no teeth. One day, they talked among themselves and decided they would ask the other animals of the rainforest to help them obtain teeth. The tambaqui, or pacu, was the first to ask. He heaved himself onto the shore and dragged himself to a tall cecropia tree, the home of the spider monkeys.

"Gentle monkeys," the pacu called. "Would you be so kind as to share some of your teeth with me?"

The monkeys screeched and chattered for a long time, and then a very old monkey replied, "You may have my teeth, for my time here is nearly at an end, and I will have no need for them." And with that, the old monkey tossed a handful of teeth down to the pacu, who quickly put them into his mouth and returned to the river. This is why the pacu now has straight teeth and eats only plants and fruit—just like the spider monkeys.

Next, the payara went ashore. He came upon a jaguar that had just made a meal of a capybara. "Fierce jaguar," said the payara, "would you ever so kindly share some of your lovely teeth with me?"

The jaguar considered this request for a moment, and then he said, "Since I have eaten my fill for a week, I will give you my teeth, for they will grow back before I get hungry again." And with that, the jaguar pulled out his two long, front teeth and tossed them to the payara, who placed them into his mouth and hurried back to the river. This is why the payara has two fangs with which to skewer smaller prey—just like the jaguar.

Next, the electric eel slithered ashore, where he was greeted by a python. "Since we seem to be cousins," said the eel to the python, "perhaps you would share some of your teeth with me?"

"I have plenty," replied the python, who shook his head and let some of his teeth fall out. "Take them," he said.

The eel put the teeth into his mouth and slithered back to the river. This is why the eel now has dozens of tiny, needlelike teeth that he uses to push prey down his throat—just like the python.

Lastly, the piranha went ashore, but he could find no one willing to share any teeth with him. He returned to the river, heartbroken and

toothless. Later, the caiman floated over to the piranha and asked, "Why are you so sad?"

The piranha told how the pacu, payara, and electric eel had all received magnificent teeth that suited them perfectly, but he had received none. "I will share my teeth with you," said the caiman with a sly smile.

"How wonderful!" exclaimed the piranha.

So the caiman removed some of his teeth and gave them to the piranha, who put them into his mouth. "They fit perfectly!" the piranha said.

"Indeed!" said the caiman—and then he promptly tried to eat the piranha.

The piranha darted away, shaken but very pleased with his new teeth. And that is why the piranha has interlocking teeth with which to shred his prey—just like the caiman.

Too Many, Too Few

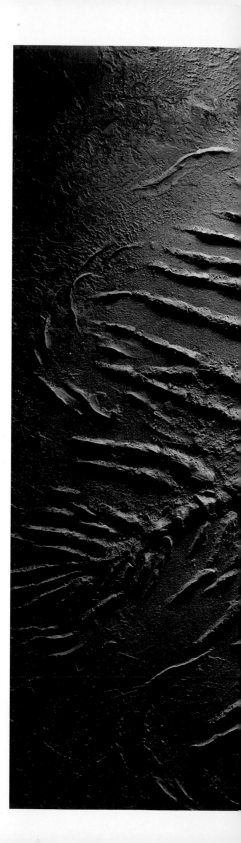

A fossil remnant of the piranha's closest known prehistoric ancestor, *Megapiranha paranensis*, was discovered in the early 1900s and tucked into a drawer in Argentina's La Plata Museum. It may have gone unnoticed if not for some housecleaning that took place in the 1980s.

Paleontologist Alberto Cione rediscovered the prehistoric fossil specimen—an upper jaw with three large, pointed teeth—and compared it with the teeth and jaw of a modern piranha. The comparison suggested that *Megapiranha*, which lived between 8 and 10 million years ago in South America, was about 3 feet (0.9 m) long.

A closer study of the teeth, which are set in a zig-zag pattern in the jaw, suggested that this fish was a vegetarian—more like the piranha cousin the pacu.

The first bony fish—ones resembling piranhas—did not appear in the fossil records until 420 million years ago.

Payaras share the piranha's river habitat and use their nearly 6-inch-long (15 cm) fangs to impale piranha, their main food source.

Wildlife management agencies are constantly on the lookout for piranhas in the United States because their existence could threaten native **ecosystems**. If piranhas should ever become established in North America, they could devastate native fish populations. Although piranhas can survive winter temperatures only in the far southern parts of California, Texas, and Florida, these fish have been found in waters as far north as Wisconsin—most likely dumped from home aquariums.

Piranhas are sometimes abandoned by their owners because these fish grow too large or become too troublesome to care for. Piranhas are messy eaters, leaving blood and bits of meat in the water that can foster the growth of toxic bacteria, so their tanks must be regularly cleaned and treated with chemicals to keep their environment healthy. The fish are also prone to illness and may need medication. Experts warn that piranhas are not a good choice for amateur aquarium enthusiasts, and piranha ownership is prohibited in at least 25 states.

While fishing in West Palm Beach, Florida, in 2009, a 14-year-old boy caught a red-bellied piranha, likely an aquarium fish that had been illegally released into the pond. The Florida Fish and Wildlife Conservation Commission (FWC) inspected the pond and found a second piranha. Since the prohibited fish can easily survive—and multiply—in Florida waters, the FWC had to take steps to prevent the possible spread of piranhas into other bodies of water.

Biologists with the Florida Fish and Wildlife Conservation Commission distributed rotenone in the affected pond.

The scientific name of the piranha that President Roosevelt saw in Brazil was originally named for him but was later renamed *Pygocentrus nattereri*.

The application of the chemical rotenone killed all the fish in the pond, including a third piranha. The chemical does not harm birds, insects, or plants, so after cleaning up the dead fish and allowing the chemical's toxic effects to subside over a period of about two weeks, the FWC restocked the pond with native fish such as bass, bluegill, and catfish. Because of the actions of perhaps one careless, law-breaking person, thousands of healthy fish had to be killed to ensure that no piranhas survived in the pond.

Despite laws prohibiting piranhas, the demand for captive piranhas is high across North America. **Captive breeding** curbs some of this demand, but many wild piranhas are captured from their native habitats and transported around the world. Most do not survive their journeys. While the exploitation of piranhas for the aquarium trade has not depleted overall piranha populations, piranhas are noticeably absent from some places where they were once abundant. Because of imbalances in their ecosystems, such as overfishing of piranha predators, piranhas have also become more numerous in places previously not densely populated by them.

For instance, a recent and sharp decline in the population of Amazon river dolphins has led to piranha overpopulation in many Amazonian habitats. Research revealed that the population of Amazon, or pink, river dolphins was

FROM "THROUGH THE BRAZILIAN WILDERNESS"

Most predatory fish are long and slim, like the alligator gar and pickerel. But the piranha is a short, deep-bodied fish, with a blunt face and a heavily undershot or projecting lower jaw which gapes widely. The razor-edged teeth are wedge-shaped like a shark's, and the jaw muscles possess great power. The rabid, furious snaps drive the teeth through flesh and bone. The head, with its short muzzle, staring malignant eyes, and gaping, cruelly armed jaws, is the embodiment of evil ferocity; and the actions of the fish exactly match its looks. I never witnessed an exhibition of such impotent, savage fury as was shown by the piranhas as they flapped on deck. When fresh from the water and thrown on the boards, they uttered an extraordinary squealing sound. As they flapped about, they bit with vicious eagerness at whatever presented itself. One of them flapped into a cloth and seized it with a bulldog grip. Another grasped one of its fellows; another snapped at a piece of wood and left the teeth marks deep therein. They are the pests of the waters, and it is necessary to be exceedingly cautious about either swimming or wading where they are found.

— by Theodore Roosevelt (1858-1919)

declining by almost 10 percent per year. However, these endangered marine mammals began to mount a comeback when a prolonged drought ended.

Human interference has affected piranha behavior as well. In 2002, reports began to emerge of piranhas biting swimmers in Brazil's Rio Tietê near the towns of Itapui and Iacanga. Researchers believe that piranha populations become isolated when dams are built on rivers. Professor Ivan Sazima, a zoologist at the State University of Campinas in São Paulo, Brazil, reported that the piranha population might have risen as much as 10 times in the 2 years after the dams were built—when the attacks began. Not having enough food in their natural diet, combined with the urge to protect their nests, likely led the piranhas to begin nipping at anything that moved in the water—including human fingers and toes. The damming of rivers has become necessary for flood protection as southeastern Brazil's human population grows. Therefore, researchers are hard at work developing strategies to relieve the tension between piranhas and humans in areas where dams have been built.

Recent research on piranha communities conducted by Anne E. Magurran, a population biologist at the University of St. Andrews in Scotland, and Helder Queiroz, a conservation biologist and fish behaviorist in charge of the Mamirauá Institute for **Sustainable** Development in Brazil, has provided some of the first evidence to dispel the commonly held belief that all piranha species form large shoals to hunt. By putting piranhas in shoals of varying sizes and then simulating attacks by water birds, the scientists were able to observe different behaviors based on the size of the shoals.

Piranhas often suffer from **parasites**, such as sea lice, chewing through their flesh, leading to bacterial infection and death.

Small shoals scattered when the predator attacked, but shoals with many members took evasive maneuvers as a group, resuming normal activity much sooner after an attack than did the smaller shoals. Escaping from a predator takes time and energy away from foraging for food, so getting back to business as soon as possible after an attack is important. Being a member of a large shoal allows a piranha to spend more time feeding and less time dashing and hiding. Magurran and Queiroz concluded that piranhas used shoals for protection rather than for ganging up on prey.

Additional research on shoaling behavior recently revealed that piranhas demonstrate a unique method of self-preservation. In large shoals, the older fish push the younger fish into the center of the group. By sacrificing older piranhas to the outer edges of the shoal and protecting the individuals most likely to reproduce, the piranhas ensure their survival as a species. With further research and education that exposes the true nature of piranhas as typical timid fish undeserving of their killer reputations, perhaps humans can help these amazing fish continue to thrive.

Glossary

amphibious – able to function both on land and in the water

archaeologist – a person who studies human history by examining ancient peoples and their artifacts

auditory – related to hearing

buoyancy – the ability to float in water

caiman – a tropical reptile related to, but smaller than, crocodiles and alligators

captive breeding – being bred and raised in a place from which escape is not possible

carcass – the dead body of an animal

ecological – having to do with the interdependence of organisms living together in an environment

ecosystem – a community of organisms that live together in an environment

endemic – native to and confined to a certain geographical location

evolve – to gradually develop into a new form

food chain – a system in nature in which living things are dependent on each other for food

indigenous – originating in or native to a particular region or country

membrane – a thin, clear layer of tissue that covers an internal organ or developing limb

omnivorous – eating both plants and animals

parasite – an organism that lives on or inside the body of another living thing

sustainable – able to be renewed or kept functioning

totem – an object, animal, or plant respected as a symbol of a group and often used in ceremonies and rituals

zoologist – a person who studies animals and their lives

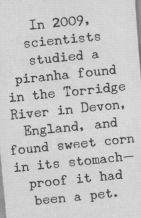

In 2009, scientists studied a piranha found in the Torridge River in Devon, England, and found sweet corn in its stomach—proof it had been a pet.

Selected Bibliography

Animal Corner. "Piranha Fish." http://www.animalcorner.org/animals/piranha-fish.

Burnie, David, and Don E. Wilson, eds. *Animal.* New York: DK Publishing, 2017.

Extreme Science. "Most Ferocious Animal Records—Piranha." http://www.extremescience.com/piranha.html.

Fact Animal. "Piranha Facts." https://factanimal.com/piranhas.

Goulding, Michael. *The Smithsonian Atlas of the Amazon*. Washington, D.C.: Smithsonian Books, 2003.

Sleen, Peter van der, and James S. Albert, eds. *Field Guide to the Fishes of the Amazon, Orinoco & Guianas*. Princeton, N.J.: Princeton University, 2018.

Index